GATEWAYS OF THE THREE-FOLD NATURE OF MAN

GATEWAYS OF THE THREE-FOLD NATURE OF MAN

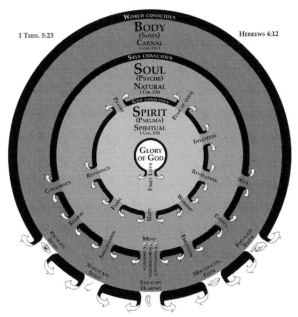

1 THES. 5:23

HEBREWS 4:12

WORLD CONSCIOUS
BODY
(SOMA)
CARNAL
1 COR. 3:1-3

SELF CONSCIOUS
SOUL
(PSYCHE)
NATURAL
1 COR. 2:14

GOD CONSCIOUS
SPIRIT
(PNEUMA)
SPIRITUAL
1 COR. 2:11

GLORY
OF GOD

THE INFLUENCE OF CHRIST EXTENDING OUTWARD TO THE WORLD

IAN CLAYTON

PUBLISHED BY
SON OF THUNDER PUBLICATIONS

Copyright © Ian Clayton
Son of Thunder Publications 2016

Second Edition

Son of Thunder Publications Ltd 2016
www.sonofthunderpublications.org

Produced by Revelation Partners
www.revelationpartners.org

Cover design by Gabrial Heath, Creative Lead, Aspect Reference Design
caleb.gabrial@clear.net.nz

Book diagrams by Adam Butterick, Third Realm Studios
www.thirdrealmstudios.com.au

Gateway diagrams by Iain Gutteridge, I.G. Design
www.ig-graphic-design.co.uk

Typeset by Avocet Typeset, Somerton, Somerset TA11 6RT
www.avocet-typeset.com

First published by Seraph Creative 2014
www.seraphcreative.org

Formatting first completed by Freedom Publishing LLP
www.freedompublishing.org

Published in the United Kingdom
for world-wide distribution

ISBN 978-1-911251-00-2

CONTENTS

INTRODUCTION

As you read this, please do not just read a part of it, as a part is only a little edge of the sword; but as you lay hold of the whole, you will be able to possess what is rightfully yours.

As a young Christian, I often wondered why I struggled with areas of my life. After deliverance, I would find freedom for a time, but I would find, suddenly, one day, all the old garbage was back in my life and there very strongly.

While meditating on the scripture "Behold, I stand at the door and knock" (Revelation 3:20, KJ21), I began to contemplate what the door or gateway really was.

This began a journey of discovery that has brought a clearer understanding of how we are supposed to function as Christians, with Christ at the centre of our being.

These are some of the keys that I have found that will enable you to be able to maintain freedom and liberty and express the Kingdom of Heaven through you to the world around you.

Gateways of the Three-Fold Nature of Man

1 Thes. 5:23

Hebrews 4:12

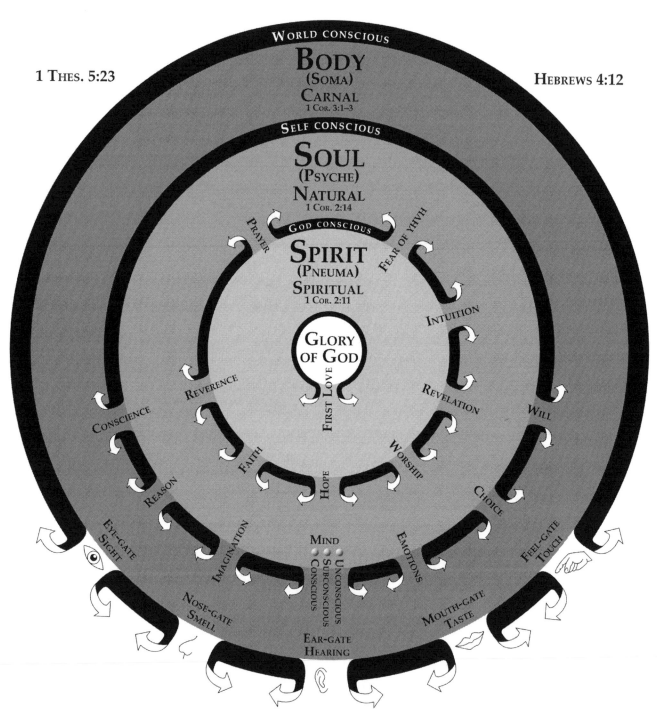

The influence of Christ extending outward to the world

Chapter 1

LAYING THE FOUNDATIONS

The human spirit is in darkness in an unbeliever. Once Christ has come to dwell inside our spirit, the spirit of man is renewed and made light with the presence of God. The renewing process starts from within and penetrates outwards.

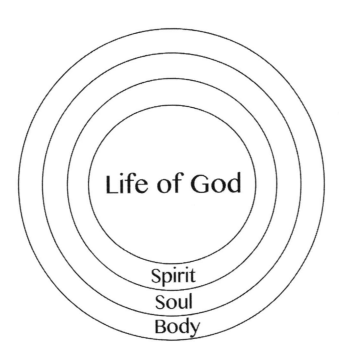

1) The centre of our being – the residing place of the promise of God, centred inside our spirit.
2) The human spirit
3) The human soul
4) The human body

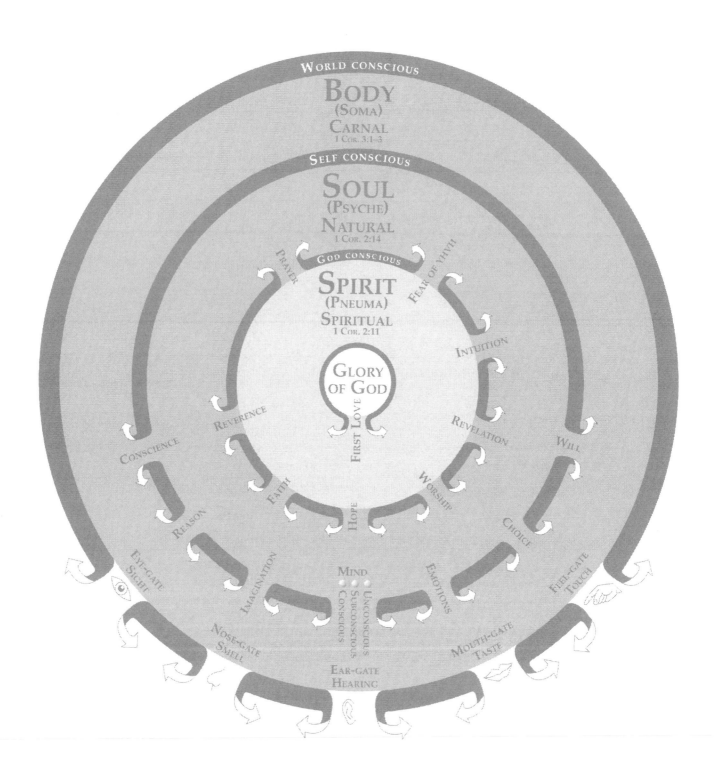

Chapter 2

GATEWAY ACCESSES

SPIRIT
Revelation : Intuition : Prayer : Reverence : Faith : Hope : Worship : Fear of God

SOUL
Conscience : Reason : Imagination : Mind : Emotions : Choice : Will

BODY
Touch : Taste : Smell : Sight : Hearing

In Genesis 2:7, the Bible says that God made man from the dust of the earth. He breathed His life into us and we became a living soul.

From the day we are born, we are trained to receive information from the gateways of the human body. These in turn affect our soul responses to the outside environment.

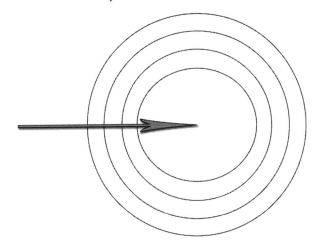

Life received from the natural world; outside to inside

This is not the way God originally made us:

"and may your whole spirit, soul, and body be preserved blameless at the coming of our Lord Jesus Christ" (1 Thessalonians 5:23).

We are a spirit being – we have a soul – and we live in a physical body.

As new, recreated beings (John 3:3, 1 Peter 1:23) the life flow should be from the inside of man outward.

The Bible tells us that for whoever believes:

"out of his belly shall flow rivers of living water" (John 7:38 KJ21).

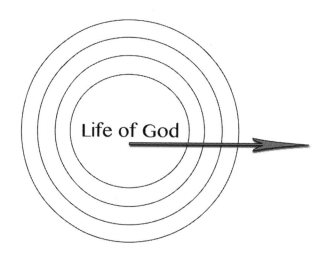

The Life of God penetrating from the inside out

Different Uses of the Gateways in the Bible

1. Business Transactions...2 Kings 7:1
2. Legal Transactions...Ruth 4:1-11
3. Criminal Cases / Disputes / Judgments..............................Deuteronomy 25:7-9
4. Proclamations..Jeremiah 17:19-20
5. Festivities...Psalms 24:7
6. Protection..2 Samuel 18:24-33
7. Tax Collections..Deuteronomy 28:50-52

Whatever action takes place in the gateways affects the city life and the individuals in that city.

The gateways are always the weakest link and need to be guarded constantly. There would always be a centurion or guard placed at these entry places. Also, tax collectors would place themselves in the gates to receive their portion of the substance of those that would come in. How like demonic spirits today.

Definition of a Gateway

A gateway is a place of authority where dominion is exercised in all its forms.

> *"For we do not wrestle against flesh and blood, but against principalities, against powers, against the rulers of the darkness of this age, against spiritual hosts of wickedness in the heavenly places"* (Ephesians 6:12).

Heavenly Place

A heavenly place is a place of power or a high place of authority where dominion is exercised. It speaks of a realm that we have legal rights to possess but do not.

We have been seated with Christ in heavenly places:

> *"(God) raised us up together, and made us sit together in the heavenly places in Christ Jesus"* (Ephesians 2:6).

A Gateway is a place of authority where dominion is exercised. As our lives have different gateways, we need to ask "What controls these gateways in our lives? Who or what has access through them?"

Whatever holds or controls your life's gateways exercises authority, dominion and control over you. This control can happen in any one of the gateways of the Soul and the Body; and for those directly involved in witchcraft/sorcery, often the spirit gateways as well.

We know that whatever we yield ourselves to, we become slaves to (Romans 6:16).

As sinners, different areas of these gateways have yielded to other spiritual forces. We have, by our actions, given them legal access and legal rights to sit in those gateways to control, dominate, and have authority over them and influence our actions and reactions.

If unrighteousness controls a gate, righteousness will have no access unless we do something to give it a legal right of access to flow through that gate.

Every time we yield ourselves either to sin or to God, we place an offering to the spiritual force that influences that area, even if we have little understanding of the process of our action or the importance of the gateway.

I realised that I had found a major key – a principle of God. Any principle of God once put into operation will work for you whether you are saved or unsaved. It is like gravity – you throw something up, and it will come down. Once it is set in motion, you will reap what you sow using that principle.

Too many Christians today sit back and expect God to do it all for them. But God is often waiting for us to act in faith. This releases His power on our behalf.

It is no good knowing something or just having a tool. The tool must be brought into action and used if any progress is to be made. To describe in simple terms the above statement:

TO KNOW about a weapon: Many people know God's Word but it has no power in them.

TO OWN it but never use the weapon: Many people know what the Bible says, but fail to appropriate it. It is like a sword. If we have it stuck in its scabbard and never use it, we only own it and it is ineffective as a weapon.

TO POSSESS and appropriate the use of the weapon effectively: This is the act of applying what we know; practising using the weapon so we know what it is like. It is the offensive action, the doing word. Taking the sword out of its scabbard and using its edge against an enemy. This is taking the Word of God and applying it effectively into our lives.

Many of us are in ignorance as to how to make a weapon effective.

"the Kingdom of Heaven suffers violence, and the violent take it by force" (Matthew 11:12).

To be violent is to take the Word of God and go in with force to dispossess in warfare what has controlled the gateways of our lives. Being violent does not imply being weak or timid. The word 'violent' means 'to use excessive force'.

These are some steps that have helped me to utilize the Word effectively:

1) Know who you are and stop agreeing with Satan when he says what you are.
2) Agree with God's Word – His Word says that I am a son of God, and that I am seated in the heavenly places. That means that you are too, if you believe it.

As spiritual beings, much of what needs to be done must be done in the spirit realm. The spirit realm has influence over and controls what happens in the natural realm, not the other way around.

As changes must flow from the residing place of God inside our spirit, let's consider the spirit faculties that are the gateways into our life.

Body Gateways

Touch, taste, smell, sight and hearing are the entry points used by demonic spirits. As they enter from outside in, you can become the temple for them to express themselves through.

I began to realize that I needed to release, somehow, the power of God from inside of me so that the life of God could be expressed through me to a world around me. So what was inside of me? The Kingdom of Heaven!

This was to become an expression outside of me as the Kingdom of God. I was to become an expression of Christ on the earth. These body gateways needed to express and reveal the glory of God. The body was not to be a place where demonic spirits were able to express themselves.

Spirit Gateways

We need to be transformed into the image of Christ. That image comes from the inside and penetrates outwards. It does not come about from external sources penetrating in. The glory needs to come from the inside of me out; but how? What must I do to release that glory – where does it flow from? How does it function and where does it start?

For something to flow, there needs to be a pathway starting from my spirit, passing through my soul and out into my body. Examining all the gateways of the body, soul, and spirit of man, it did not look complete. Not only that but it was still very hard to try to touch the glory of God in intimacy – the very presence of God inside of me.

The Lord took me to a particular scripture: "Behold, I stand at the door and knock. If any man hear My voice and open the door, I will come in to him, and will sup with him, and he with Me" (Revelation 3:20 KJ21). The Lord's desire to sup or fellowship in 'deep communion' – 'a place of deep intimacy' with us can be felt through His Words. My question to the Lord was, "But we have used that for unsaved people getting born again." How often we just accept things in the body of Christ because it has always been like that.

The Lord said to me, "That's right, but it is also for my children who are saved that need to experience deep intimacy. A person getting saved has no idea what it means to have deep intimacy. They just want their sins washed away." The Lord said to me, "This is the gateway in the deepest part of you where you touch Me and I touch you. This gateway abides in the centre of your spirit. It is expressed as first love."

This is why I have drawn the diagram as it is, with a gateway into the area of the glory of God that dwells inside of us – in our spirit. I refer to it as the veil that was torn by Christ (Matthew 27:51, Hebrews 9:3). So we are able to enter freely and have intimacy with Christ in the most Holy Place – His dwelling place in each of us, to be able to draw on Him and drink from Him.

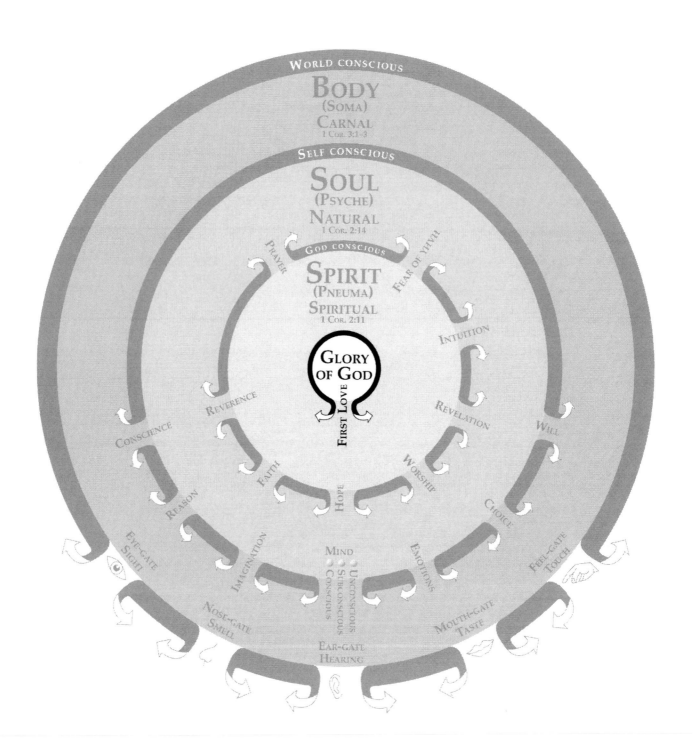

Chapter 3

THE GATEWAY OF FIRST LOVE

What is first love?

"You have left your first love…He who has an ear, let him hear what the Spirit says …. To him who overcomes I will give to eat from the tree of life, which is in the midst of the Paradise of God" (Revelation 2:4,7)

The dwelling place of God is in the centre of our being. His paradise is a place of peace and glory. Through first love, you and I have access to the tree of life. I have heard people say:

"But God put an angel with a flaming sword in that gateway so no man could eat of the tree again" (Genesis 3:24).

That flaming sword is the same fire that burns in the glory of God. So when we allow the glory fire to go through our lives, that sword cannot kill us because we have already passed through that glory and it cannot harm us. We therefore have access to the tree of life. God wants us to learn how to feed from the tree of life. There are so many Christians today who are feeding from the tree of the knowledge of good and evil, which always comes from the outside in, trying to change their behaviour, whereas the tree of life produces life from the inside out.

While thinking around this issue of first love, I realized that there is another name for it. It is called 'puppy love'. We have all been in love in this way at some time because of that first love. This I believe is one of Satan's biggest ploys in the world today. It is to cause people to close the Gateway of First Love through traumatic experience and inner vows through hurt by others. If he can close this gate, he can shut us out from being able to touch God in the centre of our being. One of the keys to unlock and unchain something is to be able to recognize what the chains are made of and then be able to deal with the issues that are associated with the chains and blocks.

Some of my own stories

I can remember being in love with a young lady and writing a love letter to her. Unfortunately, the teacher found it and read it to the class. I made an inner vow then that this would never happen again. This vow started the first links in the chain across my inner doorway of first love.

A couple of weeks later I put my hat in the refrigerator. You know – just the sort of absent minded thing done when you are in love! However, when my father found it he had a good laugh. In my heart, I put another chain on the gate.

I can remember standing by the edge of this classroom just waiting for this girl I was in love with to come past. I just wanted to see her go past and to feel the sense of fulfilment that would happen. I had some friends who stood and watched me. They started to laugh and mock, "Ha, look, he's in love." Another chain went into the gate of first love. I said inside, "No one will see me like this again."

As you may realise, I had by this stage effectively closed off the place where we are supposed to be able to touch the very presence of God – inside of us.

I was unable to get through because the gate was blocked and shut.

Finding the handle

"Behold, I stand at the door and knock. If any man hear My voice and open the door, I will come in to him, and will sup with him, and he with Me" (Revelation 3:20 KJ21).

Guess what? The handle is on your side. We must take some action to open it. Jesus stands there and knocks and waits for us to open the door. But so many of us have been so chained in this area by past experiences that the Gateway of First Love in our lives is chained and shut and therefore we are unable to have that communion with the Father in a place of intimacy.

Often, I use a very natural image to give my soul something to be able to work with when I am with God. As with the chains I had put across the entrance and chained up my gate, I needed to break them. In discussion with God over it, He told me to get some chain and wrap it around a fence post, get some bolt cutters and cut it, watch it and listen to it breaking and falling to the ground. As I was cutting, I was taking in those images and seeing the chains of my inner gateways being cut and broken away.

The Word describes Him very plainly, standing at the door. It says a door, so I stood in front of a door at my house while praying and got the image impressed in my imagination. I spent more time praying in tongues and as I stepped into that realm in the spirit, I could see the door and hear Jesus knocking on the other side of the door. But across this door were the chains of my experiences that had locked and bound me up from being able to be in love with God and would stop me from the abandonment of first love again.

In the spirit, I took my bolt cutters and the Word of the Lord.

"where the Spirit of the Lord is, there is liberty" (2 Corinthians 3:17 KJ21).

I began to break those chains in the spirit that were over my door. As they broke, I began to feel and experience the grief of what had occurred to put those chains across the doorway. So began a process of restoration: as the images would come, I would acknowledge them and then wipe them away with the Blood of Jesus. The pain that came I would allow the love of God to heal.

I could see the door but no handle was on it. I asked the Lord, "How can I open this door if there is no handle?" The Lord said that I had made myself blind to the handle because of the fear of what others would say about being in love and a fear of the love that was behind the door. He told me that only those who come and touch the door will find the handle. So I put my hand on the door, and I suddenly saw the handle.

The fire of love

Watching a clip of a movie called 'Backdraft', there is a situation where a room is so hot and full of fire, but it cannot burn because of a lack of oxygen. As the door is opened, the incoming rush of oxygen causes a tremendous explosion of fire to come through the door and into the next room.

Behind the doorway of first love is a cloud of fire that is waiting to come out and transform us into the image of the Son. Well, I did not know this stage, so I blindly opened the door and suddenly, "woosh!" I got hit by this blinding love, acceptance, and presence of God. There are no words to describe it. I fell on the floor; Jesus had come to meet with me because I had opened the door to let Him in.

Fulfilling

I suddenly found in church or at home I would be standing in meetings and I would feel inside of me this yearning and longing to just get a glimpse of Jesus and sense love is coming – it is Jesus! Just to feel His presence walk past – aren't we allowed to be in love? Especially when it is with the King of Kings! I found myself in meetings waiting for the smell of His perfume, and I would come panting after His presence.

In the Psalms, David says,

"My soul longs, yes, even faints for the courts of the LORD" (Psalms 84:2).

That yearning is first love. It is a deep desire to feel and experience the power and presence of God in reality and in intimacy.

I found myself in that euphoric feeling of being in love again. For weeks, I would just wait for Jesus to come in. This hunger built a desire for intimacy again. Out of the Gateway of First Love, you find a lover's secret: the secret things of the heart of the Father. It is from this place of the inner man that the rivers will flow.

The Bible talks about the River of God (Ezekiel 47). This river starts off as a small trickle from the source, the dwelling place of God. Guess where that place is? It is inside our spirit.

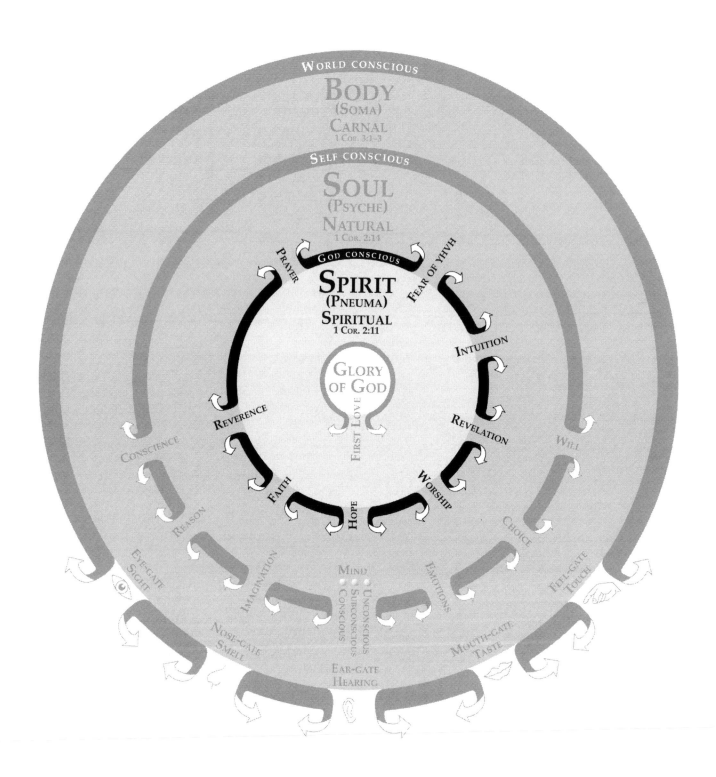

Chapter 4

SPIRIT GATEWAYS

Revelation : Intuition : Prayer : Reverence : Faith : Hope : Worship : Fear of God

These Gateways make up the nature of our spirit. It is the highest form of life referred to in the Bible as "Zoe".

In most Christians, many of these Gateways have never been opened to the Holy Spirit for the presence of God to come through. Of approximately 80% of all Christians I saw, I found only two or three gateways open and flowing with the presence of God.

Some refer to these gateways or faculties (Fear of God, Reverence, Worship etc.) as the place of communion with God. As each one has a separate function I have chosen to name them individually.

Because worship is something that is done on a regular basis it enables us to touch God in this place. Often many of us only stay at a few of our gateways. We become effective for God in only one area, whereas we need to function and flow in all these gateways to move in greater realms of authority.

It is only the measure of your freedom that dictates what is released to others. It is like a muscle that must be used to bring it into condition. If we only use one set of muscles in the natural, we get restricted and are limited to a certain way of expression – likewise in the spiritual.

How to get spirit gateways open and working

I recognised that I needed the glory of God to penetrate from the centre of my being, to flow through the gateways of my spirit to change my soul.

"For the word of God is living and powerful, and sharper than any two-edged sword, piercing even to the division of soul and spirit" (Hebrews 4:12).

1. The First Step

This is to begin to take God's Word and separate your spirit from the control and dominion of your soul. This control occurs from our birth as we are born with a spirit that does not have Christ residing in it and does not function properly in its rightful place, having dominion over the functions of the soul.

This separation is done in three ways:

a. By acting in faith
b. By praying into the dividing of your spirit from your soul
c. By yielding to the dictates of your spirit, it is useless to say that we have victory yet never appropriate the victory so that it becomes effective in our lives.

Because of the bondage our spirit is under to the soul, often people who have familiar spirits residing in their soul life, find that they receive supernatural insight into things. This occurs by the spirit sitting in a gateway of the soul and gaining access to the person's spirit gateways – usually the Gateway of Revelation. By drawing from the person's yieldedness to this spirit (usually in some form of meditation for personal covenants), the person is able to channel the destructive forces of demons through their spirit gateway. This becomes a deeper form of bondage.

As born again believers, we must yield our spirit to the Holy Spirit, for His life to flow from inside our inner being, to reflect His holiness and righteousness and to be transformed into Christ's image on the outside.

2. Opening our spirit gateways

Like any muscle if it is not used, it deteriorates until it basically becomes ineffective and useless. In the same way for the gateways of our spirit, because they have not been used, many of them are weak and small and have little influence over our soul life.

The first step is to actually open the gates of your spirit for Jesus to come in to have fellowship with you (Revelation 3:20).

"But it is not the spiritual…which came first, but the physical and then the spiritual" (1 Corinthians 15:46 AMP).

I often use a natural thing to exercise the likeness of something in the spirit realm, so that I can become effective in my prayer life.

Some simple steps

As I would open a door in the natural, so I do likewise in the spirit realm. As Christ is knocking on the other side, I would open the door or gateway for Him to come and to take possession of it in prayer. It is important that you do this on a daily basis until the flow of the anointing and your willingness to have Jesus enter via these gateways into your spirit is established. This must be done with all the gateways of your spirit. I would spend time praying in tongues and I would stand in the gateway inside my soul and spirit, open the door and welcome the glory fire to come through. We must invite the glory to come in. He will not trespass in where He is not welcome. The same way as we ask Christ into our lives, we must ask the glory fire to flow through these gateways. God will not just do it. He waits for us to yield to Him and invite Him to come.

Activation

As I started to work on the Gateway of Revelation, I would pray like this: "Father, with the fire that I have seen that came through the Gateway of First Love, I choose to open the Gateway of Revelation in my spirit. I open it and yield it to Your glory. I receive and release the power of God through this gateway, that I may begin to receive revelation of Your Kingdom that it may change my soul into the image of the Son of God who abides in me."

I found that after about twenty days of praying like this, the Word of God started to come alive. I started to see things that I had never seen before. I started to be able to look at people and perceive things I could not perceive before. The only thing that I had done was to yield to God's revelation in my spirit, to flow through the Gateway of Revelation and allow God to come through and begin to use it for His glory.

As I started to work on the other gateways of my spirit, I realized how small and dysfunctional they were. The Gateway of Worship was huge and could touch the power and the presence of God in it, but I was never able to find intimacy with God because at this stage I had never opened the Gateway of First Love.

As the gates were opened, the Lord told me to watch and see His glory make those gateways grow big. Like a little trickle of water from a spring wears a hole in the ground, and very slowly the hole gets worn open, which in turn allows more water to flow, which in turn opens the hole bigger and so on until the hole is big enough to meet the need to release the pressure that is there. This is what I found happening with the gateways of my spirit. The glory of God that came through the gateways burnt up and consumed the dross that had kept the gateways small.

One of the issues in today's society is that we like things to be instant. Well, this is not an instant process – it is a lifestyle of praying. It is not just a 'do it once and forget it'. We must work with it and walk with it. I spent approximately five years working through all my gateways like this. The reason I worked on it was because I wanted to know that it really worked for me first, to have it as a foundation within my heart.

As your spirit receives from Christ, your soul translates this for you to understand and then the soul dictates its actions to your body. Thus we become spirit directed from Christ residing in our being.

Spiritual conflict will now start to occur as we release the power of God within us to begin to change the activities in the gateways of the soul.

A key factor is that it all takes work. To plough a field requires you to put your hand to the plough and work with it until you have finished. Likewise, there is work to do in order to free our gates.

"Whatever you loose on earth will be loosed in heaven" (Matthew 18:18).

After recognizing the need for me to open and have a flow of the power of God from all my spirit gateways, I said, "Lord, a good one to start with is the Gateway of Revelation." I know this because all of us want revelation from God, but not many of us receive it. All of us want to walk in revelation because this is our spiritual food that keeps us hungry for the secrets of the heart of God. We all need revelation about Jesus Christ, His Kingdom, who He is and who we are.

The Kingdom of God is the establishing of the Kingdom of Heaven or the life of God and that being expressed through us to establish God's rule and reign on earth.

The Kingdom of Heaven is the realm where God's rule and reign are already established.

We are in the process of releasing the Kingdom of Heaven so the Kingdom of God can be seen around us.

3. Dealing with our Soul

To recap the soul gateways:

Conscience : Reason : Imagination : Mind : Emotions : Choice : Will

In Hebrews 4:12 "the division of soul and spirit" the word 'divide' or 'separate' means 'to pry apart or to force a wedge between'.

By yielding to Christ, what I have done is to put a wedge of the glory of God between my spirit and soul. I have done this so that no other force from my soul can influence or be used to access the gateways of my spirit.

The soul is the place of the most heated battle. It is the place that primarily reflects our walk with God on a daily basis. It is in our soul that almost all our problems reside. The Bible shows us that the battle is in our mind (Ephesians 4:23). This is because it is the place of our thoughts and everything that has gone on in our lives comes through the mind.

4. Taking possession of the soul

To take something back there must be a dispossession of that which has resided there. The soul is the primary place of any form of demonic spirits, blockages, and any other forms of bondage that will occur. Remember whatever controls the gateways controls the city. Likewise whatever controls the soul controls you and dictates the actions of your body. Unless some form of traumatic event has occurred in a person's life (rape, attack, accident, molestation, murder, abuse etc.), the soul gateways mentioned above are usually functioning to some degree.

"For we do not wrestle against flesh and blood, but against principalities, against powers, against the rulers of the darkness of this age, against spiritual hosts of wickedness in the heavenly places" (Ephesians 6:12).

The soul gateways are usually influenced by demonic spirits which reside there and by the sin nature. The sin nature must be crucified with Christ. Actions and reactions to certain types of stimulation can be an indication of what is controlling parts of our soul life. I have found that each individual gateway of my soul needs to be worked on. First take possession of the gateway and place Christ at the centre of it. Then yield the soul gateway to the dictates of the spirit, allowing the life and glory of God to flow through them and dictate the body's actions.

As mentioned before, often these gateways need to be cleaned up. This can be done by the Blood of Christ. His Blood is our cleaning and restoring agent. This work never stops, but as we become cleaner we are able to receive and give out more of Christ's image and life to others.

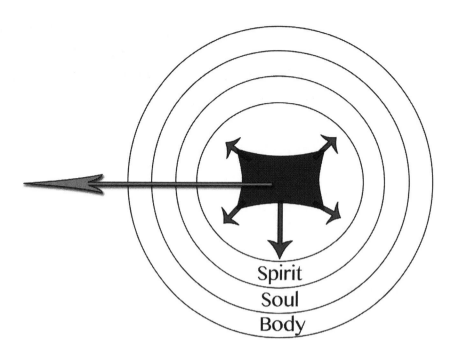

The life of Christ reflected from the inside of the spirit is free to move and be shown in my actions, firstly through my spirit, then my soul and finally my body

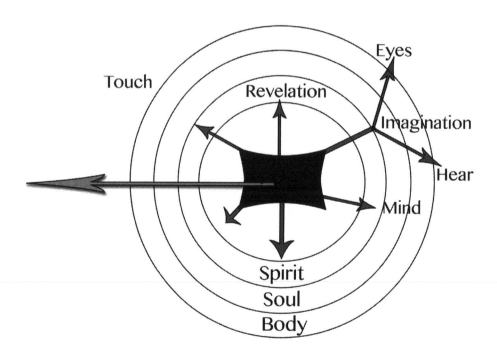

Each gateway is linked in some form to what flows from the spirit's faculties, either one or two or any combination

Often there is strong resistance on the inside of us to change. This is directly associated with demonic spirits resisting the flow of glory from our spirit into our soul. One of the keys to victory over these issues of the soul is not to give up. What a waste of time if we stand for a period of time and just before the breakthrough starts, we give in.

The Word tells us to:

"Fight the good fight of faith" (1 Timothy 6:12)

and then:

"having done all, stand!" (Ephesians 6:13).

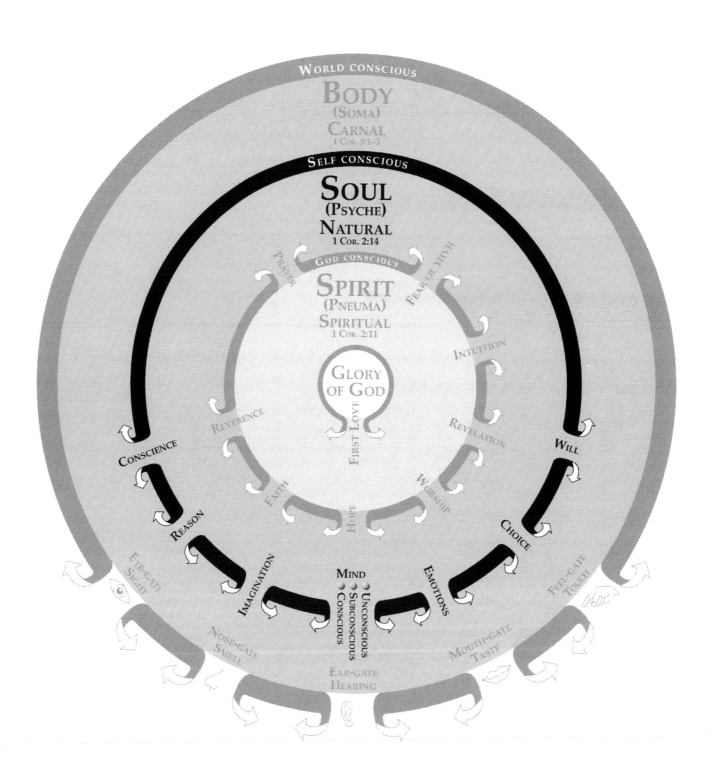

Chapter 5

SOUL GATEWAYS

Conscience : Reason : Imagination : Mind : Emotions : Choice : Will

CONSCIENCE

Some simple steps

In prayer, I brought my soul gateways into submission to the dictates of my spirit. The process and structure I went through for all the gateways of my soul, particularly the conscience, was as follows:

1) I repented of allowing demonic spirits access through these gateways of my soul.
2) Acknowledging my sin, I took responsibility for not guarding the gate.
3) I then took the Blood of Jesus by faith and wiped the gateway to make it clean and redeem it through the Blood covenant.

We must possess the gateways of our soul through spiritual warfare. Demonic spirits enter through the external gateways of the body and by us yielding to sin they latch onto areas of the soul. They do not come from the inside of us.

A simple prayer for the conscience

"Today I bring my conscience into submission to my spirit. I release the life of God to flow from my spirit, through the Gateways of Reverence and Worship and the Gateway of the Fear of God, to build a conscience of God's righteousness and truth. Where my soul has been seared by sin, I now, by faith, take the sword of the Spirit and cleave the gateway open to allow the flow of God through it to dictate my actions. Father, make me aware of my actions that I may submit to Your authority in my spirit. Today in Jesus name, I bind the spiritual force or condition that is resistant to the flow of God in me.

I loose it and cast it out of this gateway in Jesus' name. I make and place Jesus as Lord over this gateway today."

This is the type of praying that I do for the conscience gateway of my soul. The praying needs to be persistent, to enable the victory to come. During prayer like this I may become conscious of other forces operating in this and other gateways. At this stage, I would enter into warfare.

As the Conscience Gateway is re-established, the awareness of sin in our lives will also come.

Sometimes I may need to go to a brother or sister to confess the sin and have them pray for me so that I am linked into the body and do not become a 'lone ranger'. As with the spirit gateways, I choose to open the door to Jesus. I would stand in the doorway and exercise my right as an heir of God to have and hold authority over my soul gateways as the place of dominion for Jesus to reside in.

It is important to allow the Holy Spirit to lead us and quicken us in what to pray and how to pray. The conscience leads us to Godliness. If we live by the dictates of our conscience when it is not seared, we will live a holy life. Often, because the Conscience Gateway has been seared, not many of us can walk a holy life.

REASON

I found by releasing the power of God through my conscience I became aware of the holiness and presence of God. I did not just pray once into it. I worked on it and trained my conscience to begin to function the way God made it to. At times, I would pray like this:

"Father, I thank You that my Conscience Gateway is full of Your glory. I thank You that my conscience receives and releases the flow of godliness and holiness through it in Jesus name. My conscience dictates my body's actions in the world."

Very slowly I became aware of issues that God wanted me to work on.

"Yes, but this can be explained." How often do we hear this statement?

The Reason Gateway is one of the strongest places of continuous warfare with the whole area of faith. Often if a person struggles with any area of faith, it is usually an indication of a spirit controlling the Reason Gateway of the soul.

The Reason Gateway is directly linked to the Gateway of Faith. The Reason Gateway can be blocked by some of the following: self hatred, unbelief, resentment towards God or a specific unexplained traumatic experience. All of these ask the question, "But what if?"

I pray through this gateway in the following way:

"Today I bring my Reason Gateway into submission to my spirit. I release the life of God to flow from this gateway. I release the faith in my spirit to penetrate and flood into the Reason Gateway of my soul."

Again, I may need to involve in this prayer some type of spiritual warfare to dispossess any spirit that may be controlling this gateway.

IMAGINATION (Screen of the Mind)

The imagination is the single most important part of the soul as it feeds and stores everything we see, do, feel, and hear. Once this faculty or gateway is cleaned, revelations and the ability to see into the Kingdom of Heaven are heightened considerably. One of the reasons that many do not see into the realms of the Kingdom of Heaven is because of major hindrances and blockages over this area or gateway of their lives.

Dealing with the images

So many today do not deal effectively with these images.

"Bringing every thought into captivity to the obedience of Christ" (2 Corinthians 10:5).

When something is captive, it is under the will of another, and is dictated to by the one controlling that which has been captured.

What happens when images come so often? We can blame Satan and say, "Get behind me Satan," but it may not be him at all. Is it our own soul trying to maintain control, or is it God telling us to look at our heart and get it clean?

These images are already residing in us and we do not often have to make them up unless we use these first images to create fantasies. Often the substance of fantasies is from what we have heard, seen, or been involved in. These are the things that satisfy us instead of Christ meeting our needs.

Bringing a thought captive is not throwing it away and denying that it is inside us. If it is inside us, the Holy Spirit is subject to it. If we do not deal with it, we make Him subject to it!

I have found that the effectiveness in dealing with flickering images and thoughts is directly linked to our appropriation of the Blood of Jesus to them.

Some simple steps:

1) Acknowledge their presence in your life. So often we try to deny that they are there.
2) Own the sin and picture, after all it is in you and you saw it.
3) Bring it into the light (light dispossesses darkness).
4) Take the Blood of Christ and apply it to the image like a paintbrush painting over a picture.

I have found that by doing this regularly and keeping short accounts with God in my imagination, freedom comes. Once started on this path of restoration, often many more images come. As they come, steadily deal with them. It took almost one year for me to come to victory. For some people it may be longer, others may take less time. But now my imagination, the screen of my mind, is submitted to Christ and is dictated to by the actions of Christ in my spirit.

The flow of glory must penetrate the area of the imagination. I often pray for the release of glory through my spirit Gateway of Revelation, to flow into my imagination, releasing the life of God within my imagination out of my eyes that I may see into the Kingdom of Heaven.

MIND

This is one of the strongest areas that would need renewing. Often powerful bonds exist in this area.

"And be renewed in the spirit of your mind" (Ephesians 4:23).

Spirit = life of your mind; its contents; its control; its power

There are clearly three doors to the mind:

1) Conscious mind/memories
2) Subconscious mind/memories
3) Unconscious mind/memories

Each one of these areas has a different role in our lives and expression of these roles in the outworking of their content in day-to-day living. The mind also plays a major role in our dream life. Each of the areas of the mind must be submitted in prayer to your spirit, which is governed by the Holy Spirit abiding in us. I have generally found that the mind is closely linked to the two remaining areas of the soul, the will and choice. The Blood of Jesus is the cleansing agent and the Cross is the power agent to break the mind's hold over our spirit. Memories that are in our mind affect the functions of our spirit as a block and hindrance to the mind of Christ being formed in us.

"For as he thinks in his heart, so is he" (Proverbs 23:7).

It is this thinking process that needs to be changed. As our mind is brought back into submission to our spirit, the power of God in there will change our thinking. Remember that this is a process in establishing a life structure and not a quick fix to deal with sin. Sin will be dealt with as a body comes into line with the soul dictating its actions by the Holy Spirit.

Now we come to a basic summary of my journey through these passages of the mind with Christ.

The unconscious mind

Activities and actions that we do without conscious thought are the results of the unconscious mind operating. These are things that we do naturally all our lives. They are also areas that become so much a part of us that we are trained to do them without thought. It is in this area that the faculty of choice needs to be exercised to take and reshape our responses. Often demonic spirits abide in this area and we accept them and say, "Oh, it's just me…I'm like that."

Also in this area are images, situations, and actions that have taken place that we do not or cannot remember. God is able to break into this area and renew, restore, cleanse and release a person from the power of the control of the unconscious mind and any influence that may abide in or over it.

The subconscious mind

Often this area is the cause of the flickering thought life, particularly of unwanted images. The subconscious area is linked directly to the attacks of Satan through the area of imagination. The subconscious mind is described as a 'thought that is covered by a veil.' If you look at it long enough you can find detail.

Sometimes powerful bonds with demonic spirits can reside over the subconscious mind. They cause mind blocks, particularly when there has been some sort of abuse or traumatic situation or event in a person's life. Again, Jesus needs to be allowed to enter this area and then take charge. Often I have found that I needed to possess this part of my gateway in spiritual warfare for me to get access to it and also to enable the presence of God to abide there. This would result in a release of the flow of revelation and knowledge from out of those spirit gates.

Key Point: When I refer to my spirit, I am referring to the place of Christ's dwelling in me and functioning through any one of the gateways of my spirit to penetrate my soul life. I would go down the corridors of my mind declaring and wiping them with the Blood of Jesus so that everything that came before my born again experience was redeemed by the Blood and cleansed away through the covenant of adoption.

The conscious mind

The conscious mind is evident in all the daily activities that occur around us and that we do and must do. Often this is connected to our Choice and Will faculty or Gateway. The conscious mind is the area of the mind that sifts and sorts information that we receive through our entire life. Again I have found that bondage can occur here, usually via control of some form. The control either stops information, like the Word of God, going into the mind to restore it or revelation coming from our spirit to renew it. The conscious mind is the place where the germination of the seeds of God takes place. If these seeds are attacked in the conscious mind we will lose them immediately, particularly if demonic spirits reside there. Thinking patterns need to be retrained and this is the place to do that.

There is evidently a need to have Jesus residing in the conscious mind where He is Lord over it, so that the life and the Kingdom of Heaven may be reflected out of it.

I have not stopped working on this area of my mind. My goal is to "let this mind be in you which was also in Christ Jesus" (Philippians 2:5). Press in and receive the promise of God, that your mind may become an avenue to advance the Kingdom of Heaven.

Simple prayer:

"Father, today I release the glory of the Kingdom of Heaven into my unconscious, subconscious and conscious mind and into my memories to purge and clean them so that I may receive supernatural revelation from Your Word to change my life. I release the life of God through the Gateway of Revelation in my spirit like a river to flush and wash and restore my mind so that I may have the mind of Christ in me, that the actions of my body may reflect the Kingdom of God and its outworking in my actions and to those around me."

I see the mind and each area of the mind; the conscious, unconscious and subconscious mind as a great big vault where everything you have ever seen, heard, done, felt, smelt and tasted from the outside, through the gateways in your life, is stored. This includes everything from the point of conception to today. As I worked through the corridors, I would take the Blood of Jesus and I would march down each of them and paint them with the Blood of Jesus.

REMEMBER…persistence is needed!

EMOTIONS

Every emotion has a picture. The pictures are what we have stored in our life – they are the dust in our life. It is called the dust of the earth. The emotions we feel are often expressions of the pictures that we store inside our minds. When dealing with my emotions and allowing myself to feel again what I was feeling, I am really dealing with the fruit of the pictures. Often as we pray through areas of our soul, we will find a close correlation, a link between each of the soul gateways.

CHOICE

Have you ever heard somebody say, "I can't do that"? It is actually a statement that translates, "I don't know how to" or "I don't want to." Either of these indicates a blockage around the faculty of choice. The person does not have the natural knowledge of how to do something or they are making an unconscious decision that they do not want to do it. Our choice gateway gets affected from the day we are born as well as being affected by the hereditary problems of our forefathers. Faith declaration of scripture is an important part of rebuilding and energizing this gateway so that we can receive and be an expression of the Kingdom of Heaven. In this way the Kingdom of God is also received into and expressed out of our life.

Once the choice has been made to do something, then the work begins to bring that choice about. As soon as we choose spiritual direction, which is the inward choice, then the outward choice in the battle will begin to move in the right direction. Choices are part of training the soul to respond to the Kingdom of Heaven that is prompting you on the inside.

Paul says:

"I want to do the things that are good, but I do not [or cannot] do them. [For] I do not do the good things I want to do, but I do the bad [evil] things I do not want to do" (Romans 7:18-19 EXB).

By releasing the life flow of God through the gateways of your spirit the choice faculty is then possessed by the Kingdom of Heaven and right choices can be made. The conscience is closely linked to the choice gateway. The conscience is the voice that says, "I shall" or "I shall not."

THE WILL

The will says: "I will" or "I will not."

If the Gateway of the Will is under bondage to a spiritual force, it becomes ineffective when influencing the area of our choices. A person may have lived part or all of their life under the control of either a spirit or some form of human manipulation. In these situations, the will is subjected to and enslaved by that controlling influence. God has a will for our lives, and our will must be crucified and put to death so that we may do His will.

Jesus said in the garden:

"Father … not My will, but Yours be done" (Matthew 26:39 VOICE).

Having the Will Gateway submitted to the Kingdom of Heaven is of major importance if we are to truly embrace a Christian lifestyle. You and I must know the will of God for our lives. This is discovered in the Word of God. It is therefore imperative to read and become familiar with the Word of God. Reading the Word of God allows revelation of the will of God to flow from our Spirit Gateway into our Will Gateway and out into the actions of the body gateways. Again this in turn reveals the Kingdom of God to the world. The cross is often talked of as the "I" with a bridge across it. The cross is the place where the "I" dies. A principle to discovering what controls your will is to examine the scripture in Isaiah 14:12-14. It is the voice of Satan saying "I will." When doing this, be open to the prompting and convictions of the Holy Spirit that lead us to the cross.

In all of the soul gateways, you may, to some degree or other, come into conflict with demonic spirits. They will need to be dispossessed and cast out of the individual gateways. Then the life of God can be released into them. Give Him the right to possess these gateways.

As I prayed through each of my soul gateways, a release into greater areas of anointing and understanding occurred.

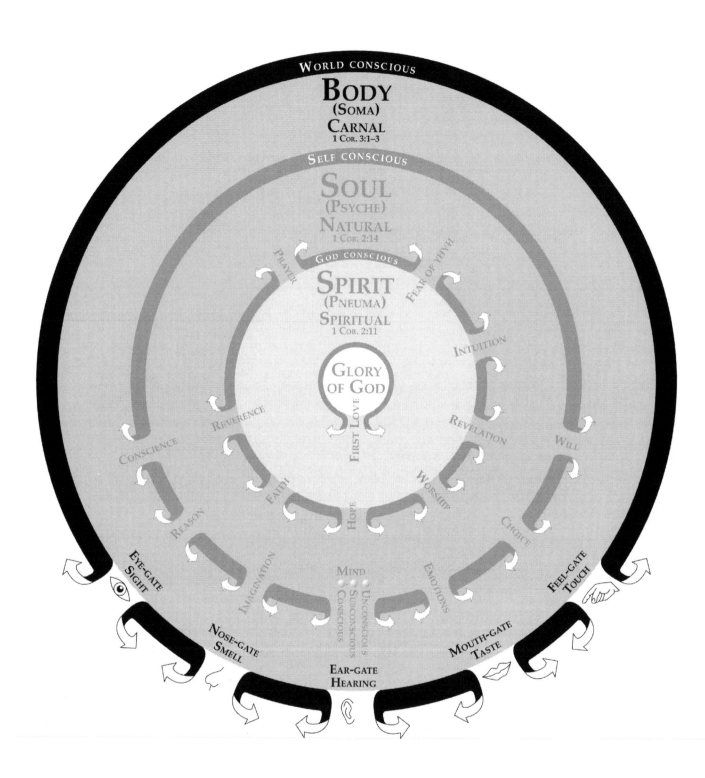

Chapter 6

BODY GATEWAYS

Touch : Taste : Smell : Sight : Hearing

With unbelievers almost all of the flow of information that is received is via the five body gateways. They constitute what is described as the carnal or natural man. Many of these gateways are influenced in one way or another by demonic spirits or just pure desires that are known as works of the flesh. Some common areas that are seen include:

TOUCH

If a person has been molested, raped or physically abused this gateway is generally defiled. The reactions of people when they are hugged can give a key to what is sitting in this gateway. It is not the person who reacts but a spirit that sits in this gateway and causes the behavioural response to the touch of love.

A person who has been physically beaten in some way may have a spirit of anger sitting in the touch gateway. This anger will control and influence the entry point of love.

When I started to pray for a person in this condition, I could hear the spirit in their touch gateway saying that their father was nasty to them and that they hated him. It had a right to be angry with him. These whispers came right from the pit of hell.

Wherever Jesus went, He touched people and the love of God flowed through Him.

In these situations, I would pray like this: "Today in Jesus name I reject the lies in this gateway. I reject the power and control over the gate of touch. I take authority in this gateway and release the fire of God to come and fill this gateway."

People can feel love flowing when the touch gateway is clean. There will be no threat in it. Others will feel safe and secure.

Ladies particularly can tell when a spirit of lust is in the gateway of touch of a guy. When they come to hug or get close to a lustful spirit, a wall will go up. They get this 'yuk' feeling in the pit of their stomach. A man can feel exactly the same thing when there is a seducing spirit sitting in the touch gateway of a woman. Some men are drawn to this without being aware of what it is that attracts them. Women with a seducing spirit can have a following of men, like male dogs to a female dog in heat, because the gateway is defiled and unclean.

TASTE

All we need is to get a scent of a freshly baked cake and our taste buds go wild. Often many who are addicted to nicotine, alcohol, food and such like find this to be one of the strongest areas to cleanse.

SMELL

As mentioned above, we often associate smell with a particular kind of food substance. Many of us are affected by the Smell Gateway more than we realise.

One of the ways to disrupt and dislodge a spirit that makes its demands through this gateway is fasting. I found that by setting a regime of fasting you can find a greater liberty.

SIGHT

The typical type of bondage in this area has to do with lust and pornography and related material. Once this gate has been defiled a strong resistance needs to be placed over it, because often a familiar spirit would then sit over this gate and control what goes in.

When going past some unclean pictures or magazines, there can be a strong pull to just look at the images. The strong pull can be a demon spirit wanting to be satisfied with the weakness in the related area.

When I first began to pray into the gateways of my body, I found that there were not even doors over them that I could close because of the sin that I had been involved in and the things that I had grown up with.

The little whispers heard, "do this; look at that; no one will know", these are demonic spirits that control the ear and Hearing Gateway. This gateway directly controls the mind gateway. Remember that the influence is from the outside in.

When people say they see things that are not there, it is because of this type of influence over the Sight Gateway that portrays the image into the imagination.
Simple prayer for the Eye Gateway:

"Father today in the name of Jesus I release the flow of the glory of God, through the Gateway of First Love and the Gateway of Revelation, into the Gateway of my Imagination and out through the

Gateway of my Eyes, that I may see into the Kingdom of Heaven with renewed spiritual sight. May my eyes become like a flame of fire to the demonic spirit world as I reflect the glory of God from the inside of me."

Seeing in the spirit is not some big full-on spiritual encounter, but rather a fruit of the way we were made to be by God. We are supposed to 'see' what is inside our spirit.

When growing up we are trained to see from the outside in. But God wants us to learn to see from the inside out.

Jesus said,

"the Son cannot do anything on his own, but only what he sees the Father doing; whatever the Father does, the Son does too" (John 5:19 CJB).

Because Jesus was seeing from the kingdom perspective, He was seeing what the Father was doing. It will be the same for us. This becomes a life flow from the Spirit of God to see the Kingdom of God flowing around us.

Seeing in the spirit is not a hard thing. It is a process of retraining our gateways to receive from the inside out, not to receive the information that the body gateways are sending in. Because we are so used to receiving from the outside in, the muscles on the inside are weak. It is a battle to learn, to train and to receive information from the inside out.

HEARING

Verbal abuse of any kind affects this gateway, allowing a spirit of rejection and death to use the gate to wreak havoc over the believer's life – the destruction associated with the little lies and whispers we hear.

The Hearing Gateway of the body very much affects the mind. It controls what the mind thinks and resists hope flowing from the spirit.

Like gears of a motor interlock and work together, each of the gateways of the body, soul and the spirit fit into one another. All our spirit gateways should have a free flow into all the gateways of our soul and then all the gateways of our body.

As the power of God is spoken and released through each of the gateways change will occur.

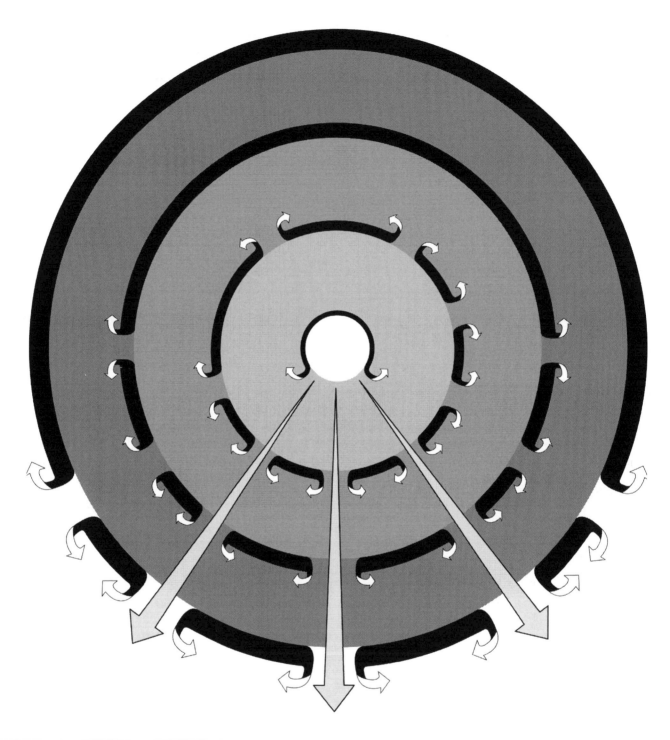

Flow is from the spirit to the soul and through to the body.

"With the mouth confession is made unto salvation" (Romans 10:10 KJ21).

We must speak salvation to each of these gates and allow the glory to flow from inside out so that we may be changed into His image from the inside out.

It is amazing to find how much the body gateways are affected and influenced in one way or another by demonic spirits. These are only a few areas that I have experienced in ministry as well as in my own life. One key to remember throughout is that these gateways are closely linked with one another, and therefore, when one is affected, usually one or two others are as well.

Examples:

SEXUAL ABUSE: Touch – Sight – Hearing are usually always affected in some way or another
ADDICTIONS: Taste – Smell – Sight are usually affected areas

The Bible tells us to put to death the works of the flesh (Romans 8:13), and this is done by the cross.

This is the only way to deal with these outside gateways. Having done this, the requirement is to build Godly desires, allowing the flow from your spirit, to penetrate these gateways and change their responses and behaviour patterns.

Remember a key principle: The body is the slave and the servant of the soul; the soul is the slave and servant of the spirit; the spirit is the slave and servant of Jesus Christ in the centre of our being.

Most of the gateways in our lives have been affected to some degree or other. I have found it important to couple fasting and prayer together while I actively go around pulling down the strongholds in the gateways of my life. This gives way to more godly desires from our spirit. It is one part of the journey to liberty.

When I came to an area that required persistence, it would take four to six months to gain true freedom.

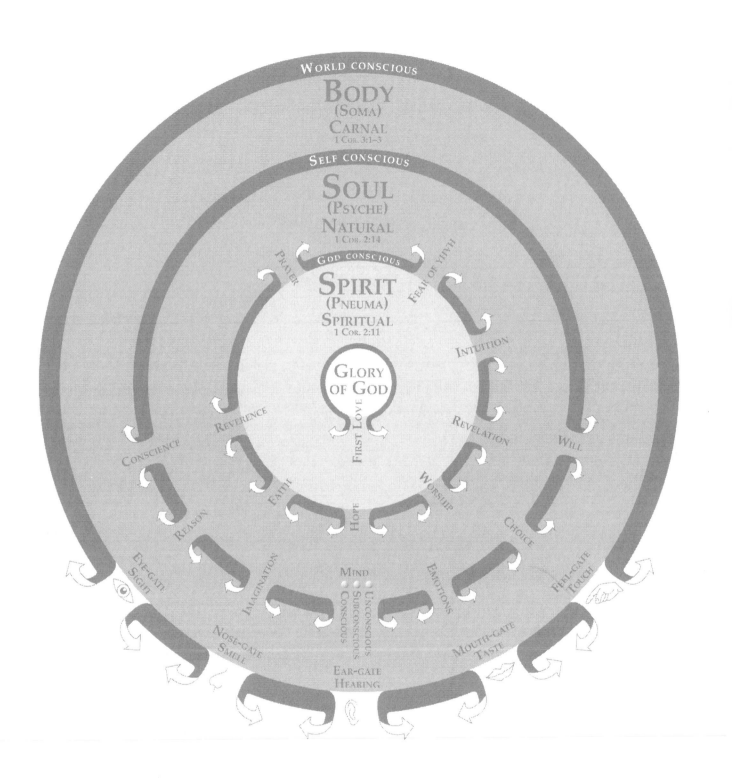

Chapter 7

KEEPING GATEWAYS OPEN

Remember this must become a way of life and not just a quick fix.

Once a gateway through which the Kingdom of God is flowing has been cleared the application of some simple keys will help the fountain of life to keep flowing.

Keep short accounts

Do not wait for a day or week to go by without applying the Blood and going through the process of repentance. When the conscience picks up an area of sin, deal with it as soon as possible. This is very important, to keep the gates clear. As you learn to fight and take possession of the gates you will find that sin has no hold on you.

Be sensitive to the Holy Spirit

Be alert to the feeling that the Holy Spirit is working. This usually starts with conviction. If condemnation comes in, it may indicate that something has been missed. We must make a conscious choice to yield ourselves to God the Father to correct us and chastise us. Once a habit of response is formed, it becomes an easier task to actually respond. When I first started, I found that I would struggle with areas of my life, until, like Jonah, I finally yielded to His higher purpose.

Spend time strongly praying in tongues

This is one of the most important aspects of spirit life to maintain the level of flow of the spirit.

The flow of the power and glory and Kingdom of God is supposed to be from our lives, from the realm of God's rule in us, to the realm of establishing His rule outside of us through our body gateways. An easy way to check this is to look at the fruit of your life. Does it represent the Kingdom of Heaven or is it something else?

When war is needed, war! When we are dispossessed of something, how can we treat the robbery nicely or kindly? When love is needed, love! We must fight with love or war for our inheritance!

A key to effective prayer: When we pray, the mind can wander.

"And if a house is divided against itself, that house cannot stand" (Mark 3:25).

We are referred to as a temple, a dwelling place of the Holy Spirit (1 Corinthians 6:19). I therefore have found it of the utmost importance to get as many of the faculties of my spirit, soul and body to function together while I pray. One of the issues facing the body of Christ today is the whole way we are trained by the Holy Spirit.

After working on issues over the gateways, I found references in scripture to the Seven Spirits of God, including:

Spirit of Might
Spirit of Wisdom
Spirit of Understanding
Spirit of the Fear of the Lord

In Isaiah 11:2 there are Seven Spirits of God mentioned. In Revelation, these Seven Spirits of God are sent out into all the world.

Like you, I ask questions from the Holy Spirit. As I began to search into these Seven Spirits of God, I discovered that the adoption process that the Bible speaks about is based on the old Roman laws. A person adopting someone into their family needed to have seven witnesses' signatures on the statement of adoption as people who would have an influence over the person's life in training the child to be presented to the world as the son and heir of the head of the family. The child would need to go through the training period first, and as development occurred, the child would be raised in stature in the family until he was able to replace the parent and carry the full weight of responsibility for the family matters.

When a transaction was done through adoption from one family to another the judge would take a damp rag and wipe the parchment of the old life of the one being adopted into the new family. In those days the ink used did not have acid or oil in it to make it permanent.

When they wiped the parchment, the name and all it contained was obliterated, wiped off and totally made clean. All their past life ceased to exist. In court, any information about the person's old life was cancelled and could never be recalled again. It was like they did not exist before their adoption.

This is like us. We need to take the rag with the Blood of Christ on it and wipe our lives. We must actively do this. Although it has already been done in the spirit, we must appropriate and keep it actively operating in our lives. It is no good just knowing about it. We must apply it and make what God has already done for us work.

The seven witnesses we have on our adoption papers are the Seven Spirits of God mentioned in Isaiah 11:2. These are the Seven Spirits I draw around my life and which I choose to allow to flow through my spirit. I hear people saying and calling on all sorts of other spirits to operate through and around them, which are the fruit of the Seven Spirits of God.

A warning: In the occult all sorts of demonic spirits are called on that produce the same kind of effects. Because something has been done by others who are mature or in leadership positions does not mean we can do the same. I make a point of always checking the Word of God. Function in what you know and then allow God to teach you the rest. In our ignorance as children, God, in His mercy and grace will cover us and help us to grow up to become sons of God.

The Seven Spirits of God that are talked about very clearly are the Seven Spirits I actively draw around my life to train me for the purpose of the Kingdom of Heaven. There is a Spirit that is first mentioned in Isaiah 11:2. It is called the Spirit of the Lord. This is not the Holy Spirit. The Holy Spirit is God, whereas the Spirit of the Lord is one of the Seven Spirits that dwell before the throne of God (Revelation 1:4). The Spirit of the Lord teaches us about the dimensions of the rule of the Kingdom of Heaven and trains us to rule as princes of the Kingdom of God. It trains us to exercise the authority and power of the Kingdom of Heaven. The Spirit of the Lord also teaches us about the throne room of God.

All the other six Spirits of God train and teach us in different aspects of Kingdom principles and how to enable them to function around us. They are basically instructions to us for the purposes of the Kingdom as sons and heirs to the throne of God. I have found that the Seven Spirits of God become a flow of life from the Kingdom of Heaven inside me to the world around me. They have become my trainers in the spirit, soul and body.

The Word says that the glory will be revealed through the veil which is to say the flesh (Romans 8:18, Hebrews 10:20). There will come a day when we will be translated from inside out. So many of us are looking for the glory to come from the outside in, but it will come from the inside out. One of the reasons we want to look for the manifestation of the glory of the Kingdom of God on the outside is because that is the way we have been trained to function by the old nature. But the Kingdom of Heaven is in us, and we need to allow it to flow from inside to the outside and manifest as the Kingdom of God around us. God will do it through us, in us, and for us if we allow Him to.

I have found that it helps when I am praying to build scriptural pictures in my imagination to help keep my soul captivated.

When our forefathers did not have water supplied like we have today, they had to get their water from a well. On the wells were pumps. When they first started to use the pump, they would get water full of sand and grit. As they continued to pump, the water would become cloudy and then suddenly it would be clear. This is a picture of what occurs in our lives. When we first start to push into these gates, a flow that is full of junk starts…but, it will clear up! Perseverance is needed. We must prime the pumps of our lives and allow the glory to flush us from the inside out. This then, becomes a flow of life-giving water to a thirsty and dry people who need the power and the presence of God.

One of the first keys we must recognise in our role and responsibility to exercise authority and rule is in the gates of our own lives. It is our role to exercise and release the Kingdom of God from the gates that are in our lives.

We do not wrestle with our flesh, we wrestle with demonic spirit beings (Ephesians 6:12) who hold our flesh to them and use it to fulfil their purpose; yet, so many of us fight with it.

"I will do this today … I will not do this today." The moment we say, "I will" or "I will not," we set ourselves under the law and put ourselves in a position of failure. The change must come from the inside out. As the flow comes from the inside out, we find that the body has no interest in the garbage of sin, because what had been the food source has been washed away.

"Lift up your heads O you gates" (Psalms 24:9).

The Bible indicates very clearly that we are a gate for the Kingdom of God to flow to the world around us. When each of us is walking in a place of freedom, then we can come together and we get a compounding effect and we create an open heaven by just being together. God is waiting for us to lift up our heads as gates for the Kingdom of God to flow through. When this happens, we will find that revival starts in a city because of the open heaven.

Simple steps to possession of all the gates of the body, soul and spirit

1) Lay hold of the gates by faith as our inheritance, so that we use our God given right to exercise dominion and authority in the gates of our lives.

2) Cast out any spirit that exercises its authority in those gates. A demonic spirit will fly its flag over the gates of our soul and body and declare that it is lord and master if we give them the opportunity to establish themselves.

3) Begin to enforce the Kingdom of God from the point of authority in the spirit, into the soul, and then into the body and then into the world. There is a battle going on for the places of authority between us and the kingdom in darkness. Any principle that has foundation can also be applied to other aspects of life.

As we have examined the gates of the body, soul and spirit the same principle can be applied to many other areas:

a) Consider the family. The family has a spirit life, a soul life and a body life.

b) A church has a spirit life, a soul life and a body life.

c) A city has a spirit life, a soul life and a body life.

Either sin or righteousness is expressed through the body life, depending on what influences and controls the gateways of each. Through the body of any group, there will be an expression of what is controlling them. God has given us the authority as sons to exercise dominion in these gates. He has given authority to stand and exercise the Kingdom from these places. The battle is ours. God has already won it, we just have not caught up with Him yet. The day Jesus looked down and said, "It is finished" (John 19:30 KJ21). He gave us the victory to hold the authority over these gates. The only reason that demons are in these gates is because we have allowed them to be there through lack of knowledge or understanding in how to pray and deal effectively with these issues.

Let's consider the aspect of nations. What controls the body life expression of a nation? What controls the soul life expression of a nation? What controls the spirit life expression of a nation? God is going to begin to rank us with the authority to take these gates over nations. It is our legal right as sons to take authority and go into these places. It is then that nations will be under the dominion of the Kingdom of Heaven. But first the places in our own life must be dealt with.

"you will be My witnesses, first here in Jerusalem, then beyond to Judea and Samaria, and finally to the farthest places on earth" (Acts 1:8 VOICE).

This means first in you and your family life, then the church and city life and then in the nation's life.

Do not expect to take a nation until you have taken a city.

Do not expect to take the city unless you have taken your church. Do not expect to take your church unless you have taken your family. Do not expect to take your family unless you have taken your own gates. It starts in you and develops outward, not from the outside in.

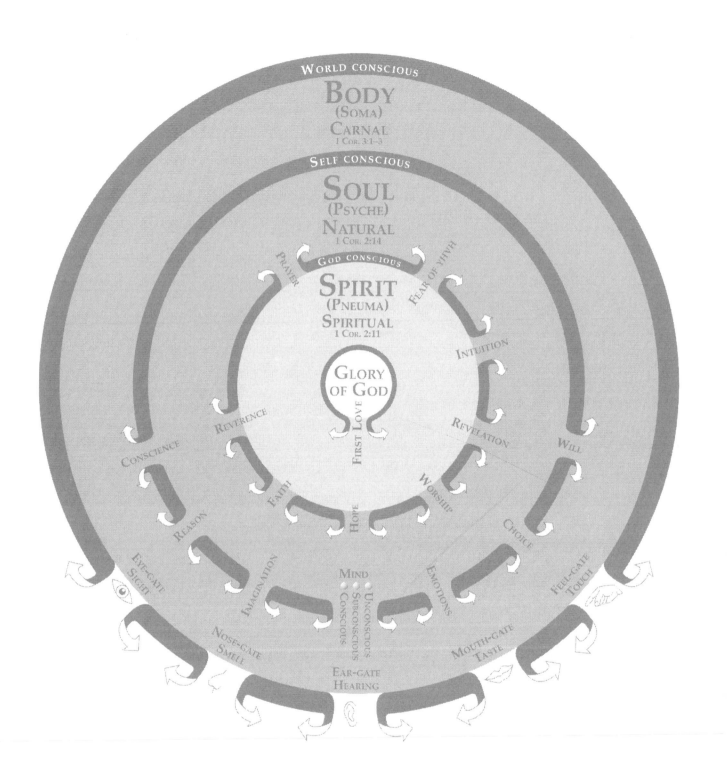

Chapter 8

SEVEN DISCIPLESHIP GATEWAYS

These gateways are ways of learning. They are intrinsic in all their aspects of learning.

As young children growing up, we experience circumstances that cause blockages that are generally spiritual in origin but affect us in the way we relate to learning and the way we actually teach others.

These blocks are usually expressed in attitudes that are displayed in the average person, such as:

"I hate school."

"I'm too old to learn."

"I cannot study."

"I find it difficult to study."

"I switch off when it comes to seminars etc…"

There are many examples of these. They are reflections of peoples learning experiences. In much of Jesus' teaching and right through Scripture, more than four or five of the gates are used at any one time.

Let's identify these gates:

1) MUSICAL: The ability to create and identify complex patterns of sound, as used by musicians.

For further study on this subject see Howard Gardner's book *Frames of Mind: the theory of multiple intelligences*

2) INTERPERSONAL: The ability to communicate effectively with others and to empathize as exemplified by facilitators and therapists.

3) INTRAPERSONAL: The ability to create personal goals and plans. To be reflective.

4) KINESTHETIC: The ability to use physical intelligence with sensitivity to movement.

5) VISUAL/SPATIAL: The ability to visualize a future result, as used by strategic planners, photographers etc. Usually very sensitive to surrounding environments.

6) LINGUISTIC: Skills with words, able to learn orally and communicate effectively with word pictures.

7) MATHEMATICAL/LOGICAL: Analytical and ability to come to a conclusion by use of logic.

The diagram below gives a much clearer idea of the way these gates are used to penetrate the body gateways. The more they are used in any given circumstance the more impacting the result will be on a student's life.

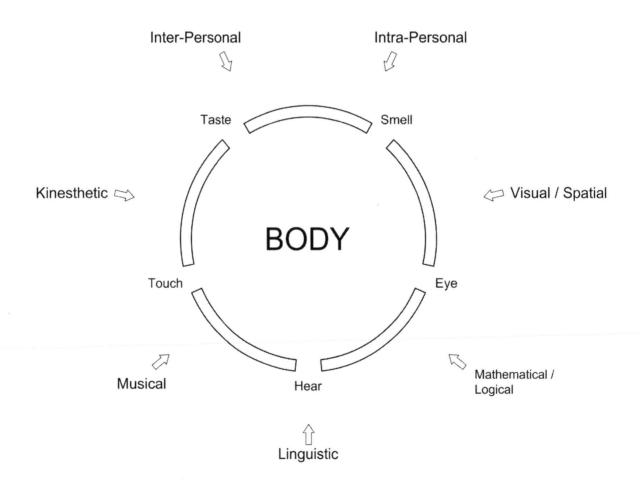

INTRA-PERSONAL

Identifies personal barriers/attitudes to learning. Uses affirmation/pat yourself on the back. Plan to teach another/specify personal learning goals. Visualise the end result/ success. Identify personal goals and values, allows time for personal reflection. Uses wall charts for peripheral learning.

INTER-PERSONAL

Teach someone else. Brainstorm in groups. Devise team strategies. Work/revise/discuss with a partner. Give/receive instructive feedback. Encourage networking, buddy and mentor relationships. Gives learners different things to listen for in lectures.

KINESTHETIC

Make a model act it out/role play. Teach someone else, write out key points. Demonstrate techniques. Draw diagrams/charts, uses mind maps. Walks around and is expressive with body language.

VISUAL / SPATIAL

Create a vision, create a map. Visualize events and outcomes. Learns from videos, etc. Diagrams, charts illustrations, colour highlights. Draw/paint a picture. Clarify/define in endless detail.

MUSICAL

Writes jingles, raps or songs. Listens for patterns and rhymes. Uses background music for study or presentation. Records key points on audio using background music.

LINGUISTIC

Discuss, write a story. Describe it to another as you read. Tape record summary. Negotiates/ describes out loud. Create a mnemonic. Seeks analogue/simile. Put in own words.

MATHEMATICAL / LOGICAL

Sequential. Flow chart and diagram. Analyze situations or information. Identify underlying problems and creates systems to solve it. Compare/ contrast/measure.

About Ian

Ian Clayton is the founder of Son of Thunder Ministries and passionately pursues a life of understanding and getting to know who the person of God really is.

Ian travels itinerantly by invitation throughout New Zealand, Africa, America, Europe and Asia ministering, teaching, equipping and mandating people to become sons of God.

Ian's heart in founding Son of Thunder is to have an avenue to put strategies and keys into believers' hands to enable them to actively participate in the reality of the realms of God's Kingdom and to experience the empowerment of life as the spirit beings we were created to be.

Ian trains and equips believers to give their lives in a persistent, passionate pursuit of the person of God, enabling them to discover that their lives are about the preparation for oneness and unity with God for the purpose of becoming mandated and authorised ambassadors of His Kingdom.

His passion is to reveal to the sons of God the purpose of the power of the attorney of God within them, removing the sense of powerlessness and hopelessness that is often attached to many in the body of Christ when they are confronted with the reality of the spirit world that surrounds them.

www.sonofthunder.org

Bible Translations used with thanks

Seven Discipleship Gateways:
Son of Thunder Publications acknowledges with thanks Howard Gardner's research.
For further information see: *Frames of Mind: the theory of Multiple Intelligences* by Howard E. Gardner, copyright © 1993. adapted for inclusion by permission of Basic Books, a member of The Perseus Books Group.

www.sonofthunderpublications.org